RAND

Background and Theory Behind the Compensation, Accessions, and Personnel Management (CAPM) Model

John Ausink, Jonathan Cave, Manuel Carrillo

Prepared for the
United States Air Force and
the Office of the Secretary of Defense

Project AIR FORCE *and* **National Defense Research Institute**

Approved for public release; distribution unlimited

The research reported here was sponsored by the United States Air Force and by the Office of the Secretary of Defense (OSD). The research was conducted in RAND's Project AIR FORCE, a federally funded research and development center sponsored by the United States Air Force under Contract F49642-01-C-0003, and in RAND's National Defense Research Institute, a federally funded research and development center supported by the OSD, the Joint Staff, the unified commands, and the defense agencies under Contract DASW01-01-C-0004.

Library of Congress Cataloging-in-Publication Data

Ausink, John A.
    Background and theory behind the compensation, accessions, and personnel
management (CAPM) model / John Ausink, Jonathan Cave, Manuel Carrillo.
        p. cm.
    "MR-1667."
    ISBN 0-8330-3428-6 (pbk.)
    1. United States—Armed Forces—Recruiting, enlistment, etc.—Mathematical models.
2. United States—Armed Forces—Pay, allowances, etc.—Evaluation. 3. United States—
Armed Forces—Personnel management—Mathematical models. 4. Employee retention—
United states—Mathematical models. I. Cave, Jonathan A. K., 1951– II. Carrillo, M. J.
(Manuel J.), 1949– III.Title.

UB323.A94 2003
355.6'1'0973—dc21

                                                                            2003010697

RAND is a nonprofit institution that helps improve policy and decisionmaking through research and analysis. RAND® is a registered trademark. RAND's publications do not necessarily reflect the opinions or policies of its research sponsors.

© Copyright 2003 RAND

All rights reserved. No part of this book may be reproduced in any form by any electronic or mechanical means (including photocopying, recording, or information storage and retrieval) without permission in writing from RAND.

Published 2003 by RAND
1700 Main Street, P.O. Box 2138, Santa Monica, CA 90407-2138
1200 South Hayes Street, Arlington, VA 22202-5050
201 North Craig Street, Suite 202, Pittsburgh, PA 15213-1516
RAND URL: http://www.rand.org/
To order RAND documents or to obtain additional information, contact Distribution Services: Telephone: (310) 451-7002; Fax: (310) 451-6915; Email: order@rand.org

Preface

This document provides details of the models of individual behavior in the Compensation, Accessions, and Personnel Management (CAPM) system[1] and is intended to convey the structure of the reenlistment and accessions models to analysts and programmers. It is one of three RAND reports that describe the CAPM 2.2 software. The other two documents are *Users' Guide for the Compensation, Accessions, and Personnel Management (CAPM) Model* (MR-1668-AF/OSD) and *A Tutorial and Exercises for the Compensation, Accessions, and Personnel Management (CAPM) Model* (MR-1669-AF/OSD). Much of what follows is fairly detailed and technical; however, we hope that the presentation is clear enough to improve understanding of some modeling fundamentals and to assist in future improvements of the CAPM model.

The initial research for CAPM was sponsored by the Assistant Secretary of Defense (Force Management and Personnel) from 1991 to 1994; follow-on work from 1999 to 2001 was jointly sponsored by that office and by the Deputy Chief of Staff, Personnel, Headquarters, U.S. Air Force. This research was conducted within the Forces and Resources Policy Center of RAND's National Defense Research Institute (NDRI) and the Manpower, Personnel, and Training Program of RAND's Project AIR FORCE (PAF). This document should be of interest to analysts concerned with the theory behind models of retention behavior.

National Defense Research Institute

RAND's NDRI is a federally funded research and development center sponsored by the Office of the Secretary of Defense, the Joint Staff, the unified commands, and the defense agencies.

Project AIR FORCE

PAF, another division of RAND, is the U.S. Air Force's federally funded research and development center for studies and analyses. It provides the Air Force with independent analyses of policy alternatives affecting the development,

---

[1]Throughout this report, "CAPM," "CAPM model," and "CAPM system" will be used interchangeably to refer to the software package as a whole.

employment, combat readiness, and support of current and future aerospace forces. Research is performed in four programs: Aerospace Force Development; Manpower, Personnel, and Training; Resource Management; and Strategy and Doctrine.

Additional information about PAF is available on our web site at http://www.rand.org/paf.

Contents

vi

Figures

Tables

Summary

Pay and other forms of compensation received for military service are important determinants of a person's decision to join the military or to reenlist after an enlistment period is completed. Since the introduction of the All Volunteer Force in 1973, understanding the effects of economic issues on the supply, recruitment, and retention of military personnel has been especially important, and determining the effects of changes in pay, retirement compensation, selective reenlistment bonuses, or selective early retirement bonuses is essential for good decisionmaking in personnel policy matters. This report describes the Compensation, Accessions, and Personnel Management (CAPM) model, which was developed to be a relatively easy-to-use personal computer–based analytical tool that would enable decisionmakers to study the effects of changes in policy on retention behavior and future inventories of military personnel.

Econometric models of the effects of compensation changes (or other policy changes that can be expressed as equivalent changes in compensation) on retention behavior usually make the simple assumption that a rational individual decides whether or not to stay in the military by comparing the potential monetary value of staying with the potential monetary value of leaving, and choosing the most lucrative course of action. Calculations of changes in retention rates in CAPM are based on one such econometric model called the Annualized Cost of Leaving (ACOL) model and a modification called the ACOL 2 model. The mathematical derivations of both models and the advantages and disadvantages of each are described in Section 2 of this report. Additionally, the simplifying assumptions made to incorporate ACOL 2 parameters in CAPM are described (in Section 3). Examples in Appendix A outline some of the limitations of these assumptions by showing when CAPM may overestimate the effects of compensation changes when compared with a "true" ACOL 2 approach.

Jonathan Cave originally called CAPM an "architecture" because it is not simply a computer model; it is an Excel®-based analytic structure that includes databases, modules written in Visual Basic for Applications (VBA), a graphic user interface, and a variety of tools to analyze model output.[1] These features are described in order to show how ACOL values are calculated, how ACOL

---

[1]Throughout this report, "CAPM," "CAPM model," and "CAPM system" will be used interchangeably to refer to the software package as a whole.

values are used to project inventories, and how CAPM can be used for policy analysis.[2]

This report concludes with a discussion of the dynamic retention model (DRM), an intuitively satisfying model of retention behavior that is computationally more difficult than the ACOL or ACOL 2 models (see Section 4). When CAPM was originally developed, the DRM was considered too difficult to implement as a desktop tool. However, recent RAND research is exploring new approaches to the DRM that may make the incorporation of a DRM-based module practicable in future versions of CAPM.

---

[2]More detailed examples of how CAPM can be used can be found in the CAPM tutorial and exercises, MR-1669-AF/OSD.

Acknowledgments

Jonathan Cave and Manuel Carrillo of RAND developed the first version of CAPM in research conducted from 1990 to 1994. Saul Pleeter, William Carr, and Lieutenant Colonel John Vetterlein, who were all in the Office of the Assistant Secretary of Defense for Force Management Policy at the time, provided invaluable assistance and support during the initial development phase. This document collects and reorganizes the theoretical work of several professionals in the field of retention behavior and provides some details of the model developed by Cave and Carrillo. Some of the material was presented to a discussion group in Santa Monica in July 1999, during which Sue Hosek, Jim Hosek, Dick Buddin, Michael Mattock, Bruce Orvis, and Al Robbert provided important comments to improve the presentation. Craig Moore, director of Project AIR FORCE's Manpower, Personnel, and Training program, made many valuable editorial suggestions. We are grateful to Glenn Gotz and Michael Mattock, who served as reviewers for this work. Their insights and suggestions greatly improved the final version of this document.

Acronyms and Abbreviations

ACOL	Annualized Cost of Leaving
CAPM	Compensation, Accessions, and Personnel Management
DRM	Dynamic retention model
ETS	End of term of service
FY	Fiscal year
TERA	Temporary Early Retirement Authority
VBA	Visual Basic for Applications
YOS	Years of service

1. Introduction

Background

Ever since the introduction of the All Volunteer Force in 1973, economic issues surrounding the supply, recruitment, and retention of military personnel have been important areas of study for the Department of Defense and for each service. Developing mathematical models of retention behavior to determine the potential retention effects of changes in retirement compensation, selective reenlistment bonuses, or selective early retirement bonuses is essential to helping policymakers make the right decisions in personnel policy matters.

The basic idea behind econometric models of employee departure behavior is simple: A rational individual facing a decision about leaving current employment compares the stream of income from staying to the stream of income from leaving and decides to stay if the first is larger than the second. There are many variations on this theme. Among them are the following.

The Treatment of Income

How does the individual value income? Is "straight" income all that matters, or is income the argument of a utility function such as $U_t(w_t) = w_t^\alpha$, where w_t represents income and α is a parameter for risk aversion? How does the individual value future income—that is, what is his or her discount rate? Should it be assumed or estimated?

The Treatment of Observable Non-Income Factors

Factors besides income may affect an individual's decision to stay in or leave current employment. Among them are observable factors (sex and race) that vary by individual but not over time, and observable factors (unemployment rate, for example) that vary over time but not by individual. Still other observable factors could vary by individual *and* over time. How should these factors be included in an individual's calculations for decisionmaking?

The Treatment of Taste and Uncertainty

Unobservable factors may affect the decision to leave current employment. For example, individuals may have varying "tastes" for their current employment, so that different people with the same potential income streams may make different decisions. Their tastes might persist over time, or they might change. A decisionmaker may also face random "shocks" (such as illness or winning the lottery) that will affect the decision to stay or leave. The shock may be completely unexpected with its effect persisting over time. On the other hand, the possibility of future shocks may be known, and an individual might take this possibility into account when making a career decision. How should these potential error terms be included in a model of decisionmaking behavior?

The Treatment of the Decision Process

One approach to making the decision to stay or leave is to guess and compare expected income streams for the two options. A more sophisticated approach would involve guessing the likelihood of future decision options and figuring out what decision now would make it more likely to have opportunities to make good decisions in the future. How should the decisionmaking process be modeled?

There is a large body of literature related to modeling retention behavior in civilian and military organizations. Goldberg (2001) and Warner and Asch (1995) have good bibliographies for subject matter beyond the modeling issues discussed in this report.

Objectives and Approach

The motivation for the development of the Compensation, Accessions, and Personnel Management (CAPM) system[1] was to provide a theoretically sound, relatively easy-to-use analytical tool that would enable decisionmakers to quickly study the effects of changes in personnel policy using a personal computer. CAPM includes databases, a reenlistment model, an inventory projection model, a graphic user interface, and a variety of tools to analyze model output. A crucial component of such a tool is the underlying econometric model that relates changes in compensation to changes in reenlistment rates, and, as is usually the

---

[1]Throughout this report, "CAPM," "CAPM model," and "CAPM system" will be used interchangeably to refer to the software package as a whole.

case, the development of CAPM required certain trade-offs between model capabilities and ease of implementation.

CAPM calculations of changes in retention rates are based on a modification of the relatively simple Annualized Cost of Leaving (ACOL) model called the ACOL 2 model. CAPM makes some simplifying assumptions in order to allow rapid analysis of a variety of policy changes, and we will discuss below how CAPM uses the results of an ACOL 2 estimation in its calculations.

Organization of the Report

Section 2 starts with a detailed mathematical description of the ACOL model and discusses some of the limitations of its use in predicting the effects of changes in compensation on retention behavior. While the CAPM software is designed for the analysis of enlisted retention behavior in the Air Force, the mathematical description could be applied to the other military services and civilian employment as well. Next, the ACOL 2 model is described in order to show how it overcomes some of the biases inherent in the ACOL formulation. CAPM uses coefficients from an ACOL 2 model estimation to adjust retention rates but does not actually perform ACOL 2 model calculations, so the simplified approach CAPM uses (called the Delta method) is described.

Section 3 discusses the structure of the CAPM software and how different functions fit together. This discussion is very general; unlike the underlying retention model, there is no detailed mathematical theory for other CAPM functions.

Section 4 introduces the dynamic retention model (DRM), an intuitively appealing but computationally difficult model that overcomes many of the weaknesses of the ACOL and ACOL 2 models and has other desirable features. When CAPM was first developed, the DRM was considered too difficult for a desktop tool, but recent RAND research is exploring new ways to implement the DRM that may make its use in future versions of CAPM practicable. The section begins with a non-technical discussion of the model structure and then describes the model mathematically using the same notation used in the ACOL discussion in order to highlight the differences.

Appendix A discusses potential limitations of the simplified Delta method used in CAPM by comparing CAPM predictions with ACOL 2 model predictions. After a general description of differences, two policy examples are presented: one that shows when the simplification makes little difference in predictions and one that shows when the simplified approach leads to predictions that differ more significantly from ACOL 2 model predictions.

Appendix B shows the mathematical connection between the ACOL model and the DRM: Although it is not set up as a dynamic programming model, the ACOL model can be viewed as a simplified version of the more complex model.

2. Annualized Cost of Leaving (ACOL) Models and How CAPM Uses Them

To predict the effect of changes in compensation on retention rates and hence future personnel inventories, CAPM 2.2 uses coefficients from the ACOL 2 model. This section describes the mathematical structure of the ACOL model, its strengths and weaknesses, and how the modifications in the ACOL 2 model overcome some (but not all) of those weaknesses. How CAPM uses the ACOL 2 coefficients is also described.

Notation

The discussion will use the following notational conventions, which will also be used in Section 4 for the description of the dynamic retention model:

U^S_t is the utility from staying in the current job in period t and departing at some time in the future.

U^L_t is the utility from leaving the current job at the beginning of period t.

w^S_t is the income earned in period t if an individual stayed at the decision point t.

$w^L_t(\tau)$ is the income earned in period τ if an individual left at decision point t (for simplicity, we will assume that this includes retirement income [if any] from the job that is left).

γ_i is the "taste" individual i has for his current employment net of any taste for alternate employment (in the discussion below, we drop the i to simplify the notation).

β is an individual's discount factor.[1]

ε^S_t is a random "shock" experienced if the individual stays in his current employment at time t.

---

[1] If an individual has an annual discount rate r, he expects that an investment of $100 this year will be worth $100(1 + r)$ dollars next year. Similarly, the present value of $100 payable next year is $100/(1 + r)$ this year. The discount factor is $\beta = 1/(1 + r)$.

We will also assume that an individual must leave the work force at the end of period T and that $w^L{}_{T+1}$ includes the present value of all future income (which will include any retirement pay or Social Security benefits).

With these conventions, whatever model is used for retention behavior, an individual will choose to remain with the current employer if the utility of remaining exceeds the utility of leaving:

$$U_t^s - U_t^L > 0. \tag{2.1}$$

The ACOL Model

In this model developed by Warner (1979) for a study of retention in the enlisted force, the utility of a decision is simply the present value of the income stream from that decision, and an individual is assumed to be capable of surveying the future to determine income streams from different sources. Each individual is also assumed to have a certain "taste" for the military that is expressed as the equivalent of γ dollars that are added to current income. If an individual leaves now, he or she will receive wages from the new job from now until mandatory retirement from that job. If an individual chooses to wait until a future year r to leave for a new job, he or she will receive military wages (plus the added value of the "taste" for the military) each year until year $r - 1$ and wages from the new job from year r until mandatory retirement from the new job.

The utility of waiting until r to leave and the utility of leaving now are thus given by

$$
\begin{aligned}
U_t^S(r) &= w_t^S + \gamma + \sum_{\tau=t+1}^{r-1} \beta^{\tau-t}(w_\tau^S + \gamma) + \sum_{\tau=r}^{T+1} \beta^{\tau-t} w_r^L(\tau) \\
U_t^L &= w_t^L(t) + \sum_{\tau=t+1}^{T+1} \beta^{\tau-t} w_t^L(\tau).
\end{aligned}
\tag{2.2}
$$

Wages from the new job, $w_t^L(\tau)$, are assumed to depend on both the time the individual departs (t) and the year they are being received (τ) in order to account for the benefits of military experience or the possible disadvantages of starting the new job at a later date. A person will prefer to stay with the military for now and leave at the beginning of r if

$$U_t^S(r) - U_t^L = w_t^S - w_t^L(t) + \gamma + \sum_{\tau=t+1}^{r-1} \beta^{\tau-t}(w_\tau^S + \gamma) + \sum_{\tau=r}^{T+1} \beta^{\tau-t} w_r^L(\tau) - \sum_{\tau=t+1}^{T+1} \beta^{\tau-t} w_t^L(\tau)$$

$$= \gamma \sum_{\tau=t}^{r-1} \beta^{\tau-t} + \sum_{\tau=t}^{r-1} \beta^{\tau-t}\left(w_\tau^S - w_t^L(\tau)\right) + \sum_{\tau=r}^{T+1} \beta^{\tau-t}\left(w_r^L(\tau) - w_t^L(\tau)\right)$$

$$> 0.$$

(2.3)

Expression (2.3) represents the income gain if departure is delayed until r, or how much is lost (in wages and in monetary value of "taste") by leaving now. Warner calls this amount the "cost of leaving," and a rational person will stay if the cost of leaving is greater than zero. This cost can be converted to an equivalent level annuity from year t to year $r - 1$ by dividing through by the sum from t to $r - 1$ of the discount factors. Thus, the individual will stay at least until the beginning of period r if

$$\gamma + ACOL_t(r) > 0,$$
where
(2.4)
$$ACOL_t(r) = \left[\sum_{\tau=t}^{r-1} \beta^{\tau-t}\right]^{-1} \left\{\sum_{\tau=t}^{r-1} \beta^{\tau-t}\left(W_t^S - W_t^L(\tau)\right) + \sum_{\tau=r}^{T+1} \beta^{\tau-t}\left(W_r^L(\tau) - W_t^L(\tau)\right)\right\}.$$

$ACOL_t(r)$ represents the "annualized cost of leaving" in terms of wages.[2] Now assume that the individual checks all possible future dates for starting new employment and determines the maximum value of $ACOL_t(r)$. Call this value simply $ACOL_t$. If this maximum value is not enough to make the individual stay, he will leave, so the decision to stay is made if

$$\gamma + ACOL_t > 0$$
or
(2.5)
$$\gamma > -ACOL_t.$$

If we now write the cost of leaving in period t for a person with taste γ as $c_t(\gamma) = \gamma + ACOL_t$, we can say that an individual will stay if the cost of leaving is greater than zero ($c_t(\gamma) > 0$), but he will leave if $c_t(\gamma) < 0$.

Assuming the tastes of individuals in a cohort are distributed according to the probability density function $f(\gamma)$, the probability that an individual with a given $ACOL_t$ will stay (or the proportion of individuals who will stay) in period t is

[2]In some model implementations (such as Daula and Moffit, 1995), the income differences after year $r - 1$ are neglected, so that the $ACOL_t$ value is based on income differences only from t to $r - 1$. This implicitly assumes that $W_t^L(\tau) = W_r^L(\tau)$—that is, that an individual will receive the same "new job" income in year τ regardless of when the new job was started. This disregards the possibility that income from the new job will probably depend on tenure in the new job.

$$\text{Prob}(\gamma > -ACOL_t) = \int_{-ACOL_t}^{\infty} f(\gamma)d\gamma. \qquad (2.6)$$

If the taste of individuals is distributed normally with mean μ_γ and standard deviation σ_γ then the probability of staying given in equation (2.6) is

$$F\left(\frac{ACOL_t - \mu_\gamma}{\sigma_\gamma}\right), \qquad (2.7)$$

or $\qquad \text{Prob}(\gamma > -ACOL_t) = F(\alpha_0 + \alpha_1 ACOL_t), \qquad (2.8)$

where $\alpha_0 = -(\mu_\gamma/\sigma_\gamma)$, $\alpha_1 = (1/\sigma_\gamma)$, and $F(x)$ is the standard cumulative normal distribution.

This representation makes it easy to compare the development of the ACOL model to a "classical" regression approach. Suppose individuals have an underlying choice variable y_i^* related to $ACOL_t$ values by the equation

$$y_i^* = \alpha_0 + \alpha_1 ACOL_t + \gamma_i, \qquad (2.9)$$

where the error terms γ_i account for all unknown influences on the decision to leave and are (for the sake of this example) distributed normally with mean 0 and standard deviation 1. If we assume that an individual will stay if $y_i^* > 0$, then the probability of staying is

$$\begin{aligned}\text{Prob}(y_i^* > 0) &= \text{Prob}(\alpha_0 + \alpha_1 ACOL_t + \gamma_i > 0) \\ &= \text{Prob}(\gamma_i > -(\alpha_0 + \alpha_1 ACOL_t)) = F(\alpha_0 + \alpha_1 ACOL_t),\end{aligned} \qquad (2.10)$$

which has the same form as equation (2.8).

In implementing the ACOL model, equation (2.9) is often used with the assumption that the error terms are distributed logistically, that is, with cumulative distribution function

$$g(\gamma) = \left(1 + e^{-\gamma}\right)^{-1}.$$

In this case, the probability that an individual will stay is

$$\text{Prob}(\gamma_i > -(\alpha_0 + \alpha_1 ACOL_t)) = \left[1 + e^{-(\alpha_0 + \alpha_1 ACOL_t)}\right]^{-1}. \qquad (2.11)$$

Once a method of determining future income for an individual is decided upon, calculating the value of $ACOL_t$ is fairly simple, especially since in practice an individual's discount rate is usually assumed rather than estimated. The parameters α_0 and α_1 can be found using the method of maximum likelihood—probit in the case of equation (2.10) and logit with equation (2.11). The estimated parameter α_0 is proportional to the mean of the taste distribution, and α_1 is proportional to the *inverse* of the standard deviation. Since the underlying distributions are different, of course, the estimated probit and logit parameters would be different.

Advantages and Disadvantages of the ACOL Model

Parameters in the ACOL model are easy to calculate, but there are some philosophical and theoretical concerns. First, in the ACOL model there is a slight inconsistency in interpretation. The discussion leading to equation (2.6) assumed that an individual's taste persists over time. But the "regression" formulation that leads to the probit/logit approach implicitly assumes that the tastes are independently and identically distributed over time.

As we follow a cohort over time, we would expect some people with lower taste for the current job to leave for other employment even if income incentives to remain are high. On the other hand, people with high taste for the current employment will remain despite income incentives to leave. As a result, the taste distribution is "censored" each year as people with low tastes depart. In other words, the average taste of individuals who have been on the job longer should be higher than for younger (in terms of years of employment) employees, and the variation in tastes should be lower for those who have been on the job longer.

When parameters of the model are estimated in one period, they define a taste distribution of the population. We have noted that the mean of this distribution is proportional to α_0 and that the standard deviation is *inversely* proportional to α_1. Since the population usually contains individuals from various time-of-service cohorts, the value of α_0 will be too high for the junior employees and too low for the more senior ones. Since the estimated standard deviation of the population will be too low for the junior employees and too high for the senior employees, the value of α_1 will be too high for the juniors and too low for the seniors. As a consequence, this model could underpredict the effect of changes in compensation on junior employees but overpredict the effect on more-senior employees. On the other hand, since more-senior employees will on average have a higher taste for the current employment, they will be more inclined to stay regardless of changes in compensation. Thus, in estimating the model, the tendency to stay could be attributed to small changes in the $ACOL_t$ value, and predicted effects of income changes would be biased upward.

The ACOL model's inability to deal with the censoring of tastes over time also affects its ability to forecast the effects of changes in compensation. For example, if the Air Force pays a bonus to enlisted personnel if they reenlist after their first term of service, more people with relatively low taste for the military will stay than without the bonus. At the end of the second term of service, these low-taste individuals will almost certainly leave. We would expect, then, that with the bonus, the retention rate at the end of the second term of service would be *lower* than if the bonus had not been introduced. The ACOL model cannot capture this effect.

Calculation of $ACOL_t$ assumes that individuals can determine with certainty the departure time r in the future that maximizes the ACOL value. According to ACOL logic, any proposed compensation change that does not change the maximum ACOL value will have no effect on a person's decision to leave. Changes in retirement vesting or changes in future compensation that are heavily discounted or uncertain might not change the size of $ACOL_t$. The ACOL model might, then, be incapable of predicting behavioral changes that would result from a change in military retirement packages.

A final issue with the ACOL model is how it can address observable non-income factors. It has been common practice in Department of Defense ACOL estimations to introduce these factors by adding them to the decision rule so that an individual stays if

$$ACOL_t + Z_t \delta + \gamma > 0, \tag{2.12}$$

where Z_t is a vector of individual factors (sex, race, etc.) and non-individual factors (such as unemployment rate) and δ is a vector of coefficients. Introducing individual fixed effects in this way is easy to justify, as they can be considered part of an individual's taste, and estimation of their coefficients will simply shift the mean of the taste distribution. It is more difficult to justify the inclusion of non-individual factors. For example, the unemployment rate would affect an individual's expectations of income in a new job, so its effect might be better modeled by using it to adjust the calculation of $ACOL_t$ values rather than as a regressor that would affect the taste distribution.

The ACOL 2 Model

Coefficients estimated for the ACOL model are potentially biased because of censoring of the taste distribution over time. The ACOL 2 model (see Black, Moffitt, and Warner, 1990a, and Mackin, 1996) is designed to decrease this bias by using panel data to help differentiate between the effects of individual specific tastes and additional random shocks. An individual random shock (uncorrelated with taste) is added to the utility of staying, so that the utilities of staying and leaving are

$$U_t^S(r) = W_t^S + \gamma + \varepsilon_t + \sum_{\tau=t+1}^{r-1} \beta^{\tau-t}(W_\tau^S + \gamma) + \sum_{\tau=r}^{T+1} \beta^{\tau-t} W_r^L(\tau)$$

$$U_t^L = W_t^L(t) + \sum_{\tau=t+1}^{T+1} \beta^{\tau-t} W_t^L(\tau).$$

(2.13)

Using the annualized cost of leaving defined in equation (2.4), the individual will stay if

$$\begin{aligned} &U_t^S - U_t^L > 0 \\ &\Rightarrow ACOL_t + \gamma + \varepsilon_t > 0 \\ &\text{or} \\ &\varepsilon_t > -\left(ACOL_t + \gamma\right). \end{aligned}$$

(2.14)

An individual will stay if $c_t(\gamma) = \gamma + ACOL_t > -\varepsilon_t$ but will leave if $c_t(\gamma) < -\varepsilon_t$. If $f(\varepsilon_t)$ is the probability density function of the random shock (or error), the probability of staying is

$$\int_{-c_t(\gamma)}^{\infty} f(\varepsilon) d\varepsilon.$$

(2.15)

If the error is distributed normally with mean zero and standard deviation σ_ε, the probability of staying is $F((ACOL_t + \gamma)/\sigma_\varepsilon)$, where $F(x)$ is the standard cumulative normal distribution. If we observe a person over several periods from t to $t + s$, the probability of staying through $t + s$ is

$$\prod_{\tau=t}^{t+s} F\left((ACOL_\tau + \gamma) / \sigma_\varepsilon\right).$$

(2.16)

Finally, if a cohort with individuals of varying tastes is hired in period t, and $g(\gamma)$ is the probability density function of the taste distribution with mean μ_γ and standard deviation σ_γ, then the proportion of the cohort that stays through period $t + s$ is

$$\int_{-\infty}^{\infty} \left(\prod_{\tau=t}^{t+s} F((ACOL_t + \gamma) / \sigma_\varepsilon)\right) g(\gamma) d\gamma.$$

(2.17)

Black, Moffitt, and Warner (1990a) define the following variables to assist estimation of the model and to provide insight into how it works:

$$\sigma_u^2 = \sigma_\gamma^2 + \sigma_\varepsilon^2$$
$$\rho = \sigma_\gamma^2 / \left(\sigma_\gamma^2 + \sigma_\varepsilon^2\right)$$
$$g = \left(\gamma - \mu_\gamma\right) / \sigma_\gamma \qquad (2.18)$$
$$r = \sigma_\gamma / \sigma_\varepsilon = \sqrt{\rho / (1 - \rho)}.$$

The variable ρ is the correlation in successive time periods between individual specific errors (taste) and the total error (taste plus random shock). With these definitions, the proportion of the cohort that stays through period $t + s$ can be written as

$$\int_{-\infty}^{\infty} \left(\prod_{\tau=t}^{t+s} F\left(-\left(ACOL_\tau + \mu_\gamma\right) / \left(\sigma_u \sqrt{(1-\rho)}\right) + rg\right) \right) \left(1 / \sqrt{2\pi}\right) e^{-g^2/2} dg. \qquad (2.19)$$

The term $1 / \sigma_u \sqrt{(1-\rho)}$ is the coefficient of $ACOL_\tau$. Thus,

> the coefficient rises in value as ρ rises in value. This suggests that [departures] become more sensitive to the [ACOL value] as dispersion in permanent unobservable differences among individuals diminishes, and as random factors exert less influence on the quit decision (Black, Moffitt, and Warner, 1990a, p. 249).[3]

In applications of the ACOL 2 model, it is common to add variables for observable individual characteristics as in the ACOL model, so the decision to stay is made if

$$ACOL_t + Z_t\delta + \gamma + \varepsilon_t > 0. \qquad (2.20)$$

Estimation of the ACOL 2 model is more difficult than the ACOL model because it uses panel data and it requires numerical evaluation of the integral in equation (2.19). In their study of the departure behavior of U.S. federal government employees, Black, Moffitt, and Warner (1990a) obtain maximum likelihood estimates for ρ, σ_u, and coefficients on $ACOL_t$ and Z_t.[4]

Advantages and Disadvantages of the ACOL 2 Model

Because the error structure of the model differentiates between the effects of taste and of random shocks, the ACOL 2 model accounts for the possibility that a cohort's taste distribution may change over time. Black, Moffitt, and Warner

---

[3]This is clear when one recognizes that the fraction simplifies to $(1 / \sigma_\varepsilon)$. Thus, if the variance of the random factors decreases, the coefficient increases, so in this way we can say the departures become more sensitive to ACOL values as the random factors exert less influence.

[4]Their Gaussian quadrature approach is described in Butler and Moffitt (1982); see Section 3 and Appendix A of this document for more discussion on this approach.

(1990a) found that the model provided a better fit to actual departure behavior of civil servants than did a standard ACOL approach. However, Gotz (1990) criticizes the model for some inconsistencies in interpretation. For example, an individual receives a random shock in year t, and the effect of this shock is expected to continue as an addition to the person's "utility," as in equation (2.13). In the estimation, however, the error is effectively treated as a one-time experience and comes from "outside" the model—that is, the decision to stay or leave is based on differences in income streams (the source of the $ACOL_t$ value), but the error term is simply added to the $ACOL_t$ value. The cost of leaving calculation, then, does not take into account the expected value of *future* shocks that an individual may experience. Gotz notes that even though a person expects a random shock in period t, there is no provision for the effect of new shocks in the future. Therefore, "individuals are surprised by shocks each period, but never figure out that the shocks will keep coming" (Gotz, 1990). Individuals are not treated as if they will take into account *future* uncertainties that might affect their decisions. Policy changes that leave the maximum ACOL value unchanged but could, because of random effects (such as the chances of a bad assignment), affect an individual's future decisions (and hence his or her current decision) would not have an effect on retention predictions in the ACOL 2 model.

Obtaining Retention Rates from ACOL Values

With the ACOL model, we have seen that ACOL values are related to retention rates by equation (2.8):

$$\text{Retention Rate} = F(\alpha_0 + \alpha_1 ACOL_t) = F(y), \qquad (2.21)$$

where $y = \alpha_0 + \alpha_1 ACOL_t$ and $F(x)$ is the cumulative distribution for the taste.

The change in retention rates induced by a compensation change could be obtained simply by comparing the retention rate calculated using the baseline ACOL value with the retention rate calculated using the new ACOL value.[5]

With the ACOL 2 model, calculation of retention rates for a given year is more complicated. Equation (2.19) gives the *cumulative* continuation rate from t to $t + s$. The retention rate is the probability that an individual remains through $t + s$ *given* that he had remained through $t + s$, which requires calculating the result in equation (2.19) for $t + s$ and dividing by the result for $t + s - 1$. This is obviously not as simple as it is for the ACOL model: Using the ACOL 2 model to

---

[5]CAPM has the capability of using this approach or the Delta method with the ACOL model if updated ACOL coefficients become available.

predict a change in retention rates caused by changes in compensation requires the development of a set of panel data with ACOL values for prior periods in which an individual made the decision to stay, not just the calculation of ACOL values from leaving in future periods.

However, if one accepts the idea that the ACOL 2 approach produces a more accurate coefficient for the ACOL value because it has accounted for the censoring of tastes over time, we can still use it to estimate changes in retention rates caused by changes in compensation by using the so-called Delta method.

Assume that the conditions represented by the baseline ACOL value actually produce the baseline retention rate. The Delta method begins by finding the *imputed* argument y_0 that produces the baseline rate. That is,

$$R_0 = F(y_0) \Rightarrow y_0 = F^{-1}(R_0). \tag{2.22}$$

If there is a change in compensation because of a new policy, we can calculate the new ACOL value, $ACOL_1$. The change in the argument of the distribution function is then

$$\begin{aligned} \Delta y = y_1 - y_0 &= (\alpha_0 + \alpha_1 ACOL_1) - (\alpha_0 + \alpha_1 ACOL_0) \\ &= \alpha_1(ACOL_1 - ACOL_0) = \alpha_1 \Delta ACOL, \end{aligned} \tag{2.23}$$

which implies that

$$y_1 = y_0 + \alpha_1 \Delta ACOL. \tag{2.24}$$

Thus, using equation (2.22),

$$y_1 = F^{-1}(R_0) + \alpha_1 \Delta ACOL, \tag{2.25}$$

and the new retention rate is $R_1 = F(y_1)$.

To estimate changes in retention rates that result from changes in compensation, CAPM calculates new ACOL values under the new policy, compares them with ACOL values under the "baseline" policy, and uses the Delta method with ACOL 2 coefficients estimated by the SAG Corporation (Mackin, 1996) to produce new continuation rates.[6] The Delta method cannot capture certain effects of compensation changes that the ACOL 2 method can (such as the possibility that a bonus at the end of one term might lead to *lower* retention rates in the next term), and even one-year predictions with the two methods will

---

[6]This is done in the VB_RetsII routine in Module 2 of the Visual Basic for Applications (VBA) program.

differ; the approach is simply a way to use a less biased coefficient to link changes in ACOL values to changes in retention rates.[7]

---

[7]See Appendix A for the results of numerical examples that show when the two approaches are very close and when Delta method results differ greatly from ACOL 2 results.

3. ACOL Calculations, Inventory Projections, and Steady-State Calculations in CAPM

CAPM databases contain information on Air Force enlisted personnel categorized by grade (E1 through E9),[1] sex, mental category (high or low),[2] and race. These databases include

- inventories by years of service (YOS)

- the percentage of personnel who are at the end of their term of service

- continuation rates for personnel at the end of their term of service

- continuation rates for personnel who are *not* at the end of their term of service (which are treated as reenlistment rates)

- promotion rates by grade and YOS

- pre-calculated "baseline" annualized cost of leaving values (based on fiscal year [FY] 2001 data) by YOS.

As described in Section 2, CAPM compares new ACOL values induced by policy changes with "old" ACOL values and uses the Delta method with ACOL 2 model coefficients to calculate new continuation rates. This section briefly describes how the ACOL values are calculated, how the continuation rates are used to predict changes in inventory, and how a "steady-state" population can be calculated. There is no complicated theory involved in this part of the CAPM software, but users should understand the broad outline of the computer routines.

---

[1]E1 through E9 are the nine enlisted grade classifications used to standardize compensation across the military services.

[2]"Mental category" is a technical term used for performance on the Armed Forces Qualification Test. There are eight levels of performance. For example, "The policy of accessing quality active duty enlisted personnel will be assessed by measuring the number of enlistees scoring in mental categories I, II, and IIIa on the Armed Forces Qualification Test (AFQT)," according to AF Policy Document 36-20, March 13, 2001. In CAPM, people in category IIIA and above are treated as "high" mental (or aptitude or quality) category. Those in categories IIIB and below are in the "low" mental category.

ACOL Calculations

This part of the CAPM program is simply a series of iterations over grade, sex, mental category, and race that calculate the components of pay needed to determine the ACOL value.[3] The basic steps involve the following:

- Calculation of the expected present value of the stream of civilian pay for each year that the individual could leave the military. This pay is based on years of military service, years in the new civilian job, sex, race, and mental category.[4]

- Calculation of the expected present value of the stream of retirement pay (if any) for each year that the individual could leave the military for a new job.

- Calculation of the expected military pay for each year the individual might remain in the military. This calculation takes into account promotion probabilities, involuntary separation probabilities, and a variety of pay elements (such as regular military compensation and reenlistment bonuses).

- Calculation of the value of leaving the military this year, calculation of the value of leaving in each possible future year (until mandatory retirement), and determination of the ACOL value for a given departure year. In the iteration over future departure years, if the ACOL value of a subsequent departure year is larger than an earlier departure year, the smaller value is replaced. The program thus returns the maximum ACOL value, but it does not store the ACOL values for all potential departure years. The program does not keep track of the departure year that yields the maximum ACOL value.

The output of this routine is a set of ACOL values and continuation rates by grade, sex, race, mental category, and YOS that can be displayed in a variety of ways. Table 3.1 shows a sample tabular output with the ACOL data displayed by grade and YOS. A similar table for the continuation rate of individuals at the end of their term of service can also be produced.

---

[3]These calculations are performed in the subroutine VB_ACOL_V2, located in Module 4 of the CAPM VBA project.

[4]Coefficients for the equation used in this calculation were estimated by the SAG Corporation (Mackin, 1996), and the values of the coefficients are in the CAPM users' guide, MR-1668-AF/OSD.

Table 3.1

Sample Display of ACOL Values for Air Force Enlisted Personnel
(in dollars)

YOS	E1–3	E4	E5	E6	E7	E8	E9
				Grade			
1	25,237						
2	26,777	27,557	30,400	34,203			
3	28,528	28,701	31,048	34,948			
4	28,091	28,853	30,835	34,523			
5	27,511	29,116	30,488	34,159			
6	27,523	29,655	30,521	34,253			
7	27,697	29,941	30,427	34,328	38,184		
8	26,628	30,196	30,418	34,223	37,717		
9	18,404	29,364	29,729	33,504	36,767		
10	18,112	29,975	30,433	33,334	36,815	41,757	
11			31,326	33,993	37,166	41,957	
12			33,180	35,784	38,971	43,868	
13			35,672	38,279	41,833	47,473	
14			39,485	42,191	45,959	51,773	
15			45,229	48,032	52,266	59,084	
16			61,719	65,210	70,602	80,215	
17			83,687	88,247	95,592	108,989	122,825
18			128,835	138,328	150,482	171,304	193,662
19			264,347	295,302	324,995	368,176	417,855
20			31,095	32,889	25,329	30,573	27,667
21					17,457	21,982	17,914
22					32,363	37,122	31,000
23					12,256	15,809	8,651
24					30,810	32,513	24,738
25						11,913	3,237
26						39,635	26,423
27							−4,436
28							−7,775
29							−11,120
30							−11,167

Inventory Projections

Once the ACOL values have been determined and continuation rates have been adjusted, the CAPM program projects future inventories for the number of years desired by the user. The program takes into account the desired end strength of the enlisted force, and it also allows for the possibility of other "structural" controls, such as limitations on the number of personnel in certain grades. The inventory routine is an iterative process, consisting of the following steps:[5]

---

[5]This calculation is performed in the subroutine VB_InvProjV in Module 2 of the CAPM VBA project.

- New reenlistment rates are calculated using the Delta method and ACOL 2 coefficients. If ACOL values are the same as the "baseline" values, these rates will be the same as those stored in the original database.

- Individuals in the starting inventory are promoted, using (in the first iteration) smoothed promotion rates by YOS and grade.

- User-specified prior service accessions and minimum levels of non-prior-service accessions are added, and minimum involuntary separations (severances), including any high-year tenure severances, are taken out.

- Historical continuation rates are applied to the portion of the force not at the end of a term of service.

- The ACOL-derived reenlistment rates (the continuation rates for those at the end of their term of service) are applied to the remainder of the force.

- End strength is compared with the user-specified target, and additional non-prior-service accessions or severances are performed as needed.

- The grade structure is compared with user-specified constraints and/or targets, and promotion rates are adjusted as needed.[6]

- If promotion rates were not adjusted, the model stops. Otherwise, it starts the loop again by promoting individuals using the new promotion rates.

The output of this routine is a set of inventories by grade, sex, race, mental category, YOS, and projection year. Figure 3.1 is a sample graphical display of projected inventories by YOS over a four-year period.

Costs

When the inventory is known, it is fairly simple to calculate a variety of costs associated with the size and composition of the force. CAPM produces output on the amount of regular military compensation paid, retirement liability for those who are assumed to retire, and retirement accrual.[7]

Steady-State Projections

It is occasionally useful to determine the composition of the enlisted force that would eventually result if given continuation rates did not change over time. This is called the "steady-state" force, and CAPM has a simple routine to

---

[6]Details of how this adjustment is made are found in the CAPM users' guide, MR-1668-AF/OSD.

[7]This is done in the subroutine VB_FullCost, which is in Module 2 of the CAPM VBA project.

20

calculate it.[8] Essentially, this routine determines the cumulative continuation rates at each YOS for each enlisted category—that is, the proportion of the entering force that reaches each YOS. With these numbers and a desired end strength of the force, the population distribution by YOS can be determined.

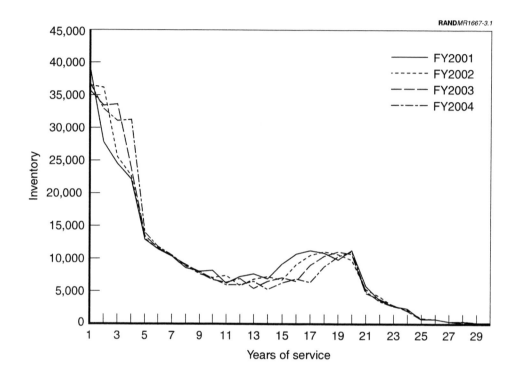

RAND*MR1667-3.1*

Figure 3.1—Sample Inventory Output

CAPM and Policy Analysis

Because of the simplifying assumptions made in order to use the ACOL 2 coefficients, forecasts using CAPM are best interpreted as potential *trends* resulting from policy changes. CAPM software is useful for policy analysis because it can reveal unexpected changes that encourage the analyst to think harder about the expected effect of a change in policy. A slightly artificial example will illustrate this point. The enlisted pay table introduced in January 2001 represented an increase in pay for all enlisted personnel, but the structure of the table was also meant to change some incentives: The rate of pay increases was slower for individuals who remained in the same grade over time than for those who advanced more rapidly. The graph in Figure 3.2 shows the result of

---

[8]This subroutine is called VB_SteadyState and is in Module 2 of the CAPM VBA project.

using CAPM to project reenlistment rates from 2001 to 2004 under the new pay table compared with reenlistment rates under the old pay table.

The "ribbons" in the figure show that at 20 YOS, for example, the higher 2001 pay table would induce a retention rate approximately 4 percentage points higher than the retention rate with the old pay table. In CAPM, this means that more people complete 19 YOS and start serving their 20th YOS. One would expect that with higher pay for all grades, retention rates would increase. The decrease in retention rates for those in their 22nd YOS in FY2001, then, comes as a surprise and might initially raise suspicion about the model. Rather than being a mistake in the model, however, the decrease is an indication of a transition of cohorts from one retirement system to another.

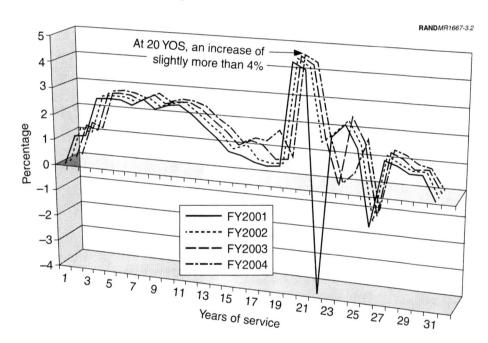

Figure 3.2—Reenlistment Rate Changes

Until 2000, there were three separate military retirement systems. For those who entered military service before September 8, 1980, retirement pay was a multiple of final basic pay. For those who entered military service between September 8, 1980, and August 1, 1986, retirement pay was based on the average basic pay for the highest 36 months of the person's career, which is usually the average of the last three YOS (hence the approach is called the "High-3" system). The Military Reform Act of 1986 created the REDUX retirement system, which also based retirement pay on High-3 basic pay but (among other changes) reduced the multiplier used to calculate retirement pay. REDUX applied to all members who joined on or after August 1, 1986. CAPM 2.2 incorporates these three systems into its calculations.[9]

In 2001, those who are in their 22nd YOS (having completed 21 YOS) entered the service in early 1980, so they are under the "old" retirement system, which is more generous than the system that applies to those who entered in 1981. For this cohort, the increase in basic pay from the new pay table makes the *retirement* benefit more valuable than before and encourages more people to leave, resulting in the decreased reenlistment rate for those in their 22nd YOS shown in Figure 3.2.

Summary

CAPM software allows a policy analyst to adjust many variables to simulate policy changes that might affect an individual's expected military compensation. The effects of these changes (if any) on ACOL values will influence continuation rates, and the potential consequences on future personnel inventories can be studied using the various ACOL, continuation rate, inventory, and cost outputs of the model.

---

[9]The National Defense Authorization Act for FY2000 made two major changes: (1) it allows those in this group to choose between the High-3 retirement system and the REDUX retirement system, and (2) it gives a $30,000 bonus to individuals who, at their 15th YOS, agree to stay in the military through at least 20 YOS and retire under the REDUX retirement system.

4. The Dynamic Retention Model

Section 2 noted some of the limitations of the ACOL and ACOL 2 models, and the introduction hinted that a more sophisticated approach to modeling decisionmaking would involve guessing the likelihood of future decision options and figuring out what decision now would make it more likely to have opportunities to make good decisions in the future. This section describes the DRM, which is one such sophisticated dynamic programming approach that is very appealing.[1] After describing the model in non-technical terms, we present some mathematical details that highlight the differences between the DRM and the ACOL approach. We also discuss some computational issues related to estimating coefficients for the DRM and similar models.

A Non-Technical Description of the Model

The DRM was developed by Glenn Gotz and John McCall in the late 1970s and early 1980s to study the behavior of Air Force officers. Following Gotz and McCall (1984) and Fernandez, Gotz, and Bell (1985), we will describe the model "from the bottom up" to highlight its major assumptions.[2]

Suppose an individual is faced with the decision of whether or not to leave the military. If he leaves, suppose he expects to receive a salary of $50. If he stays, there is a 50 percent chance of maintaining his current position with a salary of $20, and a 50 percent chance of receiving a promotion and increasing his salary to $100. These possibilities are shown in Figure 4.1.

If the individual stays, the expected payoff is $(1/2)(100) + (1/2)(20) = \$60$, a value we could associate with the circle in the figure where the chance of promotion is faced. We would expect that, other things being equal, a rational person would make the decision to remain in the military because the expected payoff of $60 exceeds the $50 payoff from leaving.

---

[1]Many modeling approaches appear in the literature. Daula and Moffitt (1995) used a model very similar to the DRM in a study of Army enlisted personnel reenlistment decisions. Stock and Wise (1990) introduced what they called the "option value" model (which is similar in some respects to the ACOL model) to analyze the effects of pension plan changes in large corporations. Ausink (1991) used the option value model to study the retention decisions of Air Force pilots.

[2]The example and Figures 4.1–4.3 are based on Fernandez, Gotz, and Bell (1985).

24

RAND*MR1667-4.1*

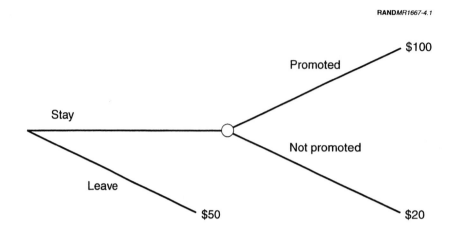

Figure 4.1—Decision Tree with One Decision Point

The same decision process can be applied if there is more than one decision point, as in Figure 4.2.

RAND*MR1667-4.2*

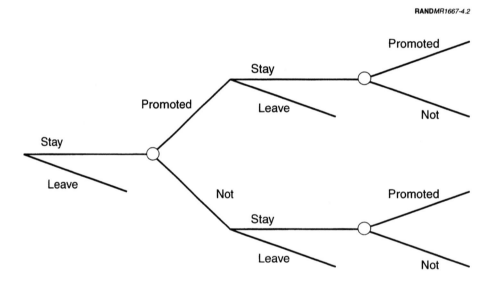

Figure 4.2—Decision Tree with Two Decision Points

In this case, if the individual stays in his current job and is promoted, he will follow the upper part of the decision tree and face another decision in the future. The best decision at the second decision point can be determined by comparing the expected payoff from staying with the payoff from leaving, so a value can be assigned to the first "promoted" branch of the decision tree. Similarly, if the individual stays initially and is not promoted, he will follow the lower part of the decision tree, where he can determine the best decision (and its value) at the second decision point by comparing expected payoffs. Thus, a value can be assigned to the first "Not" promoted branch. The best initial decision can now be easily determined because it has been reduced to the situation of Figure 4.1: Knowing the probability of promotion and working backward from possible future paths, the expected value of staying at the first decision point can be calculated and compared with the expected value of leaving.

This process is the basic idea of the dynamic programming approach and can be applied to any problem with a finite number of stages (or periods). If everything were known with certainty, an individual could use calculations like these to determine whether or not to stay in his current job or leave for a new one. It is possible, however, that random factors (such as disability or an unsatisfactory move associated with a promotion) will also affect a person's future decisions.

A decision tree with random factors is shown in Figure 4.3. If a person stays in the military and is promoted, he or she will then experience a random shock—a good one (high value of ε) or a not-so-good one (low, even negative, value of ε). The monetary value of this shock will influence the decision to stay or leave; knowing the probability distribution of the shocks allows an individual to determine its effect on the expected value of staying in the military.

With this general background about decisionmaking, we can describe some of the features of the DRM, including several behavioral assumptions about individuals and distributional assumptions about possible random effects.

First, like the ACOL models, the DRM assumes that officers are risk neutral and desire to maximize the expected present discounted value of their future income streams. This means that an individual knows how to calculate the expected value of future earnings in the civilian world and that the individual knows the probability of obtaining future promotions in the military so that he or she can calculate the expected value of an income stream from staying in the military.

Second, again as with the ACOL models, individuals are assumed to have a certain "taste" for military life that is known to the individual and is constant over time. As noted in Section 2, we would expect that over time those who dislike the military will leave in greater numbers when their enlistment periods end, and so the distribution of tastes among those who remain in the military will change: The average taste value of the population will increase over time, so as the military population ages, retention rates will generally increase. Like the ACOL 2 model (but unlike the basic ACOL model), the DRM tracks a population over time and can allow for this "censoring" effect.

26

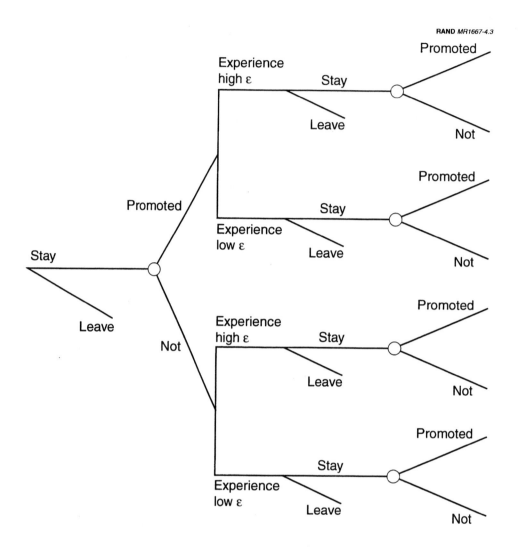

RAND *MR1667-4.3*

Figure 4.3—Decision Tree with Random Shocks

Third, individuals are assumed to experience random non-monetary shocks that have an equivalent monetary value. The probability distribution of these shocks is known to each individual and to the analyst.

In addition to these assumptions about individual behavior, Gotz and McCall (1984) make several aggregate assumptions. All officers have the same rate of time preference and thus apply the same discount rate in calculating present values. Officers have identical beliefs about the distribution of the random shocks that each one faces. Finally, the probability that an officer will hold a regular commission (rather than a reserve commission) at his first decision point is dependent upon the value of his "taste" parameter. For technical reasons related to "solving" the dynamic programming problem, Gotz and McCall also make certain assumptions about the functional form of the "taste" distribution and the distribution of random shocks.[3]

Now we can put these basic ideas into mathematical terms.

A Mathematical Description of the DRM

The DRM assumes that an individual looks ahead to possible future decisions and makes his current decision based on an assessment of the expected value of future "correct" decisions. We do not assume that the best time to leave can be determined—only that every time a decision is faced, the individual will make the best choice, the one that gives maximum utility. The utility of staying includes the utility of this year's wages and the expected utility of making the "best" decision next year. Using the notation from Section 2, the utilities from staying and leaving are thus

$$U_t^S = w_t^S + \gamma + \beta E_t(U_{t+1}) + \varepsilon_t^S$$
$$U_t^L = w_t^L(t) + \sum_{\tau=t+1}^{T+1} \beta^{\tau-t} w_t^L(\tau) \qquad (4.1)$$
$$U_{t+1} = \max(U_{t+1}^S, U_{t+1}^L).$$

This simply says that if a person stays, he or she will earn the "staying" military wage, receive the monetary equivalent of the "taste" value, accept the monetary value of the random "shock," and receive the discounted expected value of the best decision next year. If he leaves, he will receive the wage from the new job until he is required to leave the work force altogether.[4] At any time, the correct decision is to choose the option with the maximum utility, so to decide what to do, the individual compares the utility of staying with the utility of leaving:

$$U_t^S - U_t^L = \varepsilon_t^S + \gamma + w_t^S - w_t^L(t) - \sum_{\tau=t+1}^{T+1} \beta^{\tau-t} w_t^L(\tau) + \beta E_t(U_{t+1}). \qquad (4.2)$$

An individual will stay in the military if

$$U_t^S - U_t^L = \varepsilon_t^S + c_t(\gamma) > 0, \qquad (4.3)$$

where

---

[3]The taste values follow an extreme value distribution with a location and scale parameter that are the same for all cohorts. The random shocks are distributed normally with zero mean and variance σ_ε.

[4]Gotz and McCall used a more sophisticated setup for wages received from staying in the military. See Gotz and McCall (1984).

$$c_t(\gamma) = w_t^S - w_t^L(t) + \gamma + \beta E_t(U_{t+1}) - \sum_{\tau=t+1}^{T+1} \beta^{\tau-t} w_t^L(\tau). \tag{4.4}$$

The expression $c_t(\gamma)$ is essentially the difference between income received if a person stays and income received if the person leaves for a new job. For this reason, $c_t(\gamma)$ can be called the "cost of leaving" and is analogous to equation (2.3). Equation (4.3) says that a person will stay in his current job if the random shock is not bad enough to overwhelm a positive cost of leaving or if the random shock is good enough to overwhelm a negative cost of leaving. Indeed, Gotz (1990) and Daula and Moffitt (1995) have pointed out that there is an equivalence between the ACOL value and the cost-of-leaving expression derived for the DRM in equation (4.4): If there are no random shocks, setting $c_t(\gamma) = 0$ implicitly defines "the level annuity that would make a present-value-of-income maximizing individual indifferent between staying and leaving" (Gotz, 1990, p. 265). Thus, one way of looking at the ACOL model is that it is an approximate version of the DRM in which individuals ignore random shocks.[5]

The *probability* that an individual will remain in his current job is thus

$$\text{Prob}(\varepsilon_t^S + c_t(\gamma) > 0) = \text{Prob}(\varepsilon_t^S > -c_t(\gamma)), \tag{4.5}$$

which, if the random shock has distribution $f(\varepsilon)$, is

$$\int_{-c_t(\gamma)}^{\infty} f(\varepsilon) d\varepsilon. \tag{4.6}$$

If the individual is part of a cohort that is working in period t, the proportion in the cohort who remain through period $t + s$ is

$$\int_{-\infty}^{\infty} \left(\prod_{\tau=t}^{t+s} \int_{-c_\tau}^{\infty} f(\varepsilon) d\varepsilon \right) g(\gamma) d\gamma, \tag{4.7}$$

where $g(\gamma)$ is the probability density function for taste.[6]

Gotz and McCall are careful to note that retention rates in a given year may depend on the sequences of decisions in previous years. They define the "voluntary retention rate" as the probability of an individual remaining this year *given* that he remained up to the previous year:

---

[5]See Appendix B for more mathematical details on this.

[6]The random shocks are assumed to be independently and identically distributed with mean zero and standard deviation σ_ε.

$$\frac{\displaystyle\int_{-\infty}^{\infty}\left(\prod_{\tau=t}^{t+s}\int_{-c_\tau}^{\infty}f(\varepsilon)d\varepsilon\right)g(\gamma)d\gamma}{\displaystyle\int_{-\infty}^{\infty}\left(\prod_{\tau=t}^{t+s-1}\int_{-c_\tau}^{\infty}f(\varepsilon)d\varepsilon\right)g(\gamma)d\gamma}. \tag{4.8}$$

Thus, like the ACOL 2 model, the DRM has the attractive feature of being both *forward* looking (by assessing future possibilities) and *backward* looking (accounting for changes in a group's composition because of decisions made in the past).[7] Expressions (4.6) and (4.7) also highlight a key difference between the DRM and the ACOL 2 model. In the DRM, the value of $c_\tau(\gamma)$ depends on the expected value of the "best" future decisions and, thus, includes the effects of *future* random shocks. In the ACOL 2 model (in expressions [2.15] and [2.17]), $c_\tau(\gamma)$ depends on an ACOL value based on future income without a random component; the random shock is taken into account only in the current year.

Computational Issues

The structure of the DRM (especially with the more detailed assumptions used in the original version) is appealing because the decisionmaking procedure is intuitive, the error structure captures individual-specific and random elements that make sense, and the "backward-looking" ability captures expected changes in population composition over time. These appealing features, however, have the disadvantage of complicating the estimation of the parameters of the model.

The point of developing any of the models we have discussed is to use observed data to estimate parameters that will make it possible to predict the effect of policy changes, and the method most commonly used to develop these estimates is the method of maximum likelihood.[8] Suppose observations (x_i) come from a population with probability distribution $f(x, \alpha_0, \alpha_1)$, where α_0 and α_1 are unknown parameters of the distribution (there could be more parameters, of course). Assuming they are independent, the probability that a given set of N observations will be obtained from the population is

$$l(\alpha_0,\alpha_1)=\prod_{i=1}^{N}f(x_i,\alpha_0,\alpha_1). \tag{4.9}$$

---

[7]Gotz and McCall also modify the taste function, making it conditional on whether or not an individual has a regular or a reserve commission. The taste distribution $g(\gamma)$ is thus replaced with the distribution $g(\gamma\,|\,i_1)$, where i_1 is an indicator variable for the type of commission the individual has.

[8]The following discussion is based on Kmenta (1986, pp. 175–180).

This joint probability function is called the likelihood function, and the values of α_0 and α_1 that maximize it are called the maximum likelihood estimates of the parameters. In practice, the natural logarithm of this function,

$$L(\alpha_0, \alpha_1) = \sum_{i=1}^{N} \ln\big(f(x_i, \alpha_o, \alpha_1)\big), \tag{4.10}$$

is used, and the parameters that give the maximum value are those that satisfy the first-order conditions

$$\frac{\partial L}{\partial \alpha_0} = 0; \frac{\partial L}{\partial \alpha_1} = 0.$$

For example, suppose the probability that individual i stays in the military is p_i. If we observe N individuals, with n_1 staying and the rest leaving, the likelihood function for the observations is

$$l = \prod_{i=1}^{n_1} p_i \prod_{i=n_1+1}^{N} (1-p_i) = \prod_{i=1}^{N} p_i^{Y_i} (1-p_i)^{(1-Y_i)}, \tag{4.11}$$

where $Y_i = 1$ if a person stays and $Y_i = 0$ if a person leaves. The log-likelihood function is

$$L = \sum_{i=1}^{N} Y_i \ln p_i + (1-Y_i)\ln(1-p_i). \tag{4.12}$$

We saw in expressions (2.7) and (2.8) that the probability of staying in the military with the ACOL model is given by $F(\alpha_0 + \alpha_1 ACOL_t)$, where $\alpha_0 = -(\mu_\gamma / \sigma_\gamma), \alpha_1 = (1/\sigma_\gamma)$, and $F(x)$ is the standard cumulative normal distribution.[9] The log-likelihood function is thus

$$L = \sum_{i=1}^{N} Y_i \ln F\big(\alpha_0 + \alpha_1 ACOL_t\big) + (1-Y_i)\ln\big(1-F\big(\alpha_0 + \alpha_1 ACOL_t\big)\big). \tag{4.13}$$

This is a probit formulation; standard computer packages can quickly calculate the values of α_0 and α_1 that maximize the likelihood function.

For the ACOL 2 model, the likelihood function is more complicated. If $Y_{it} = 1$ means that individual i stays in period t and $Y_{it} = 0$ means that he leaves, the ACOL 2 expression (2.19) for the proportion of people who remain from t to $t + s$ (or the probability that an individual remains) can be written

---

[9]μ and σ are the mean and standard deviation, respectively, of the taste distribution.

$$p_i = \int_{-\infty}^{\infty} \left(\prod_{\tau=t}^{t+s} F\Big(-\big(ACOL_\tau + \mu_\gamma\big) / \big(\sigma_\mu \sqrt{(1-\rho)}\big) + rg \Big)(2Y_{it} - 1) \right)\left(1/\sqrt{2\pi}\right) e^{\frac{-g^2}{2}}. \qquad (4.14)$$

Finding the values of μ_γ, σ_μ, and ρ that maximize the log-likelihood function

$$L = \sum_{i=1}^{N} \ln(p_i)$$

in this case is more difficult than with the ACOL model because an optimization routine will have to be used and the determination of each p_i will require numerical integration.

For the DRM, the contribution of each individual to the likelihood function has the form in expression (4.7). While this looks similar formally to the ACOL 2 expression, the calculations are much more difficult. Calculating the probability of staying requires that the value of c_t be known. But this requires finding the probabilities of staying and leaving at $t + 1$, which from equation (4.4) in turn depend on c_{t+1}, and so forth. Thus, for each set of trial parameter values set in a computer routine to maximize the likelihood function, the entire dynamic programming problem must be worked out: Expected values of future decisions must be found by working backward ("backward recursion") from $T + 1$ and calculating probabilities at each step. In their original work, Gotz and McCall used a two-stage approach to do this. They first fixed a trial value for the standard deviation of the random disturbance (or shock) (σ_ε) and then estimated the remaining parameters by maximizing the likelihood function conditional on this value. Different values of σ_ε were evaluated until the maximum of the conditional likelihood values was reached. This approach "did not lend itself to inexpensive estimates of asymptotic errors of the parameters of the model"[10] (Gotz and McCall, 1984, p. 23). While variations in formulation of the dynamic programming problem and advances in computer technology have made the estimation less time-consuming (as in the very similar dynamic programming approach of Daula and Moffitt[11]), the DRM is still more difficult to estimate than the other models.

There is a large literature on the difficulty of estimating parameters for more-general dynamic programming problems where the number of choices available to an individual is greater than two and where random effects are more

---

[10]Parameters estimated are the variance of the random shock distribution, the location and scale parameters of the taste distribution, and the selectivity parameter of the relationship between taste and regular/reserve commissions.

[11]In work done before their 1995 article, Daula and Moffitt (1991) describe an iterative approach that results in computational savings.

complicated.[12] Keane and Wolpin (1994) and Wolpin (1996) discuss general dynamic programming problems with K possible decision options in each of T periods of time. Stern (1997a,b) and Rust (1997) also have very good summaries of this important area of research, and Mattock (unpublished) outlines a way to use simulation to make estimation of the parameters of the DRM easier.

Conclusion

This section has described the intuitive appeal of the DRM approach to analyzing an individual's decision to remain in or leave military service. While the model captures important aspects of individual behavior, its computational difficulty has discouraged analysts from using it after the initial work of Gotz and McCall. Since the goal of the developers of CAPM was to create a desktop tool that would allow rapid analysis of different compensation policies, the DRM, appealing as it was, was considered too difficult to implement, and the simpler ACOL-based approach was used. Recent RAND research is exploring new ways to implement the DRM, and if this research is successful, the modular structure of the CAPM software will make it fairly easy to replace the ACOL-based calculation of retention rates with that based on the DRM.

---

[12]The rapid increase of calculations that must be performed as the number of decision options and decision periods increases is called the "curse of dimensionality."

Appendix

A. Comparison of the Delta Method and the ACOL 2 Model

This appendix shows how predictions using the Delta method can differ from the ACOL 2 model. After describing some general numerical tests of the two approaches, we compare two specific policy examples for Air Force enlisted personnel: a reenlistment bonus and an early retirement option.

General Tests

The basic ACOL 2 expression for the cumulative continuation rate can be written

$$\int_{-\infty}^{\infty} \prod_{t=1}^{T} (F(\alpha_1 ACOL_{it} + \alpha_0 - rg_i)) \frac{1}{\sqrt{2\pi}} e^{-\frac{g_i^2}{2}} dg_i, \qquad (A.1)$$

where $F(x)$ is the cumulative normal distribution,

$$r = \sqrt{\frac{\rho}{1-\rho}}$$

and ρ is the "correlation between the total disturbance in successive time periods."[1]

Black, Moffitt, and Warner (1990a) substitute

$$z^2 = \frac{g_i^2}{2}$$

to rewrite the expression as

$$\frac{1}{\sqrt{\pi}} \int_{-\infty}^{\infty} \prod_{t=1}^{T} (F(\alpha_1 ACOL_{it} + \alpha_0 - \sqrt{2} rz)) e^{-z^2} dz, \qquad (A.2)$$

---

[1]Black, Moffitt, and Warner, 1990a, p. 248.

which allows the use of the following Hermite-Gauss quadrature formula to calculate the integral

$$\int_{-\infty}^{\infty} e^{-Z^2} g(Z)dZ = \sum_{j=1}^{G} w_j g(Z_j). \tag{A.3}$$

Using three roots for the Hermite-Gauss quadrature,[2] we

1. generated 100 random ACOL values between –$100,000 and $50,000

2. used the ACOL 2 method (with the ACOL 2 coefficients estimated by the SAG Corporation) to calculate a continuation rate in one period for the given ACOL value

3. introduced a "policy change" in the first period by increasing or decreasing the ACOL value

4. used the Delta method and the ACOL 2 method to calculate a new continuation rate, and compared the two predictions

5. used the ACOL 2 method to calculate second- and third-period continuation rates and the changes induced by the first-period policy change.

First-Period Results

Figure A.1 shows the maximum difference between first-period predictions using the ACOL 2 approach and the Delta method. For example, if there is a decrease in ACOL of $10,000 and the initial continuation rate was in the 81–100 percent range, the ACOL 2 and Delta method predictions of new continuation rates differed at most by about 5 percentage points.

In general, for *negative* ACOL changes, the ACOL 2 method predicts *smaller* decreases in continuation rates than the Delta method does. For *positive* ACOL changes, the ACOL 2 method predicts *smaller* increases in retention rates than the Delta method does.

Second-Period Results

Figure A.2 shows the changes that the ACOL 2 model predicts will be induced in the *second* period given an ACOL change in the first period—changes that the Delta method cannot pick up. For example, for initial continuation rates of 61–80

---

[2]See Carnahan, Luther, and Wilkes (1969). The Z_j values are roots at which the function $g(Z)$ is evaluated, and the w_j values are the weights attached to the function's value at those roots.

percent, a policy that causes a $40,000 *decrease* in ACOL value in the first period induces an *increase* in retention of about 8 percentage points in the second period. This is one of the strengths of the ACOL 2 model: The population that remains after such a large ACOL decrease will have a higher average taste for the military, so in the second period the continuation rate will be higher than in the base case.

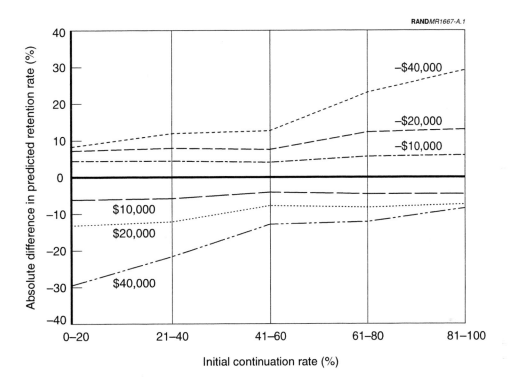

Figure A.1—First-Period ACOL 2 and Delta Method Differences

Figures A.1 and A.2 indicate that for even fairly large changes in ACOL values (on the order of $10,000), the ACOL 2 and Delta method approaches are relatively close. For very large ACOL values, the first-period predictions can be quite different—especially if the initial continuation rates are very high (with ACOL decreases) or very low (with ACOL increases).

Specific Examples

Two examples of potential policy changes that an analyst might wish to consider will help show the strengths and weaknesses of the Delta approach.

Reenlistment Bonus

FY2000 Air Force data show that there are 2,105 enlisted personnel in grade E4 (senior airman) in their eighth YOS, that 32.7 percent of them are at their end of term of service (ETS), and that the reenlistment rate for these individuals is 63 percent. Suppose the Air Force wishes to increase the reenlistment rate for this group by offering a reenlistment bonus of $20,000. CAPM shows that such a bonus would increase the annualized cost of leaving by about $6,000 (assuming a four-year reenlistment period).

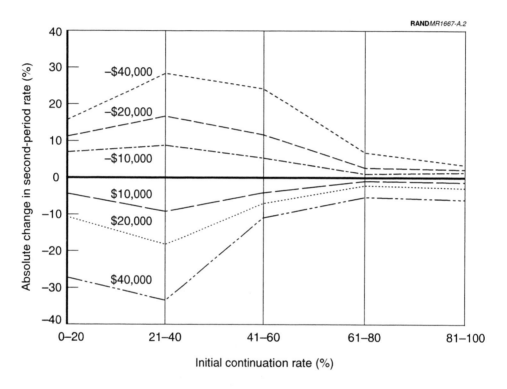

Figure A.2—Second-Period Rate Changes Caused by First-Period ACOL Changes

The first data column of Table A.1 shows that under current circumstances (the "base" case), 688 people are eligible to reenlist, and that 434 do so. This results in an inventory of 1,812 at the end of the first period. Second-period continuation rates lead to an inventory of 1,736.

The second data column of Table A.1 shows predicted changes with the bonus using the Delta method. The baseline 63 percent reenlistment rate implies a baseline ACOL value of about (–$4,800), and the $6,000 ACOL increase raises the first-period reenlistment rate to 69.56 percent.

The third data column of Table A.1 uses the same implied ACOL value (–$4,800) to calculate an ACOL 2 reenlistment rate and then determines the change that results from a $6,000 ACOL increase. Here, the change is a 4.41 percent increase, so the new reenlistment rate implied by the ACOL 2 method is 67.41 percent.

Table A.1

Effect of Reenlistment Bonus on E4s at Eight YOS

	Base	Delta Method	ACOL 2
Initial inventory	2,105	2,105	2,105
% at ETS	32.70%	32.70%	32.70%
Reenlistment rate	**63.00%**	**69.56%**	**67.41%**
Continuation rate for those not at ETS	97.30%	97.30%	97.30%
Number eligible to reenlist	688	688	688
Reenlistments	434	479	464
Number who continue without reenlisting	1,378	1,378	1,378
End of 1st-period inventory	1,812	1,857	1,842
% at ETS	16.30%	16.30%	16.30%
Reenlistment rate	**89.50%**	**89.50%**	**89.20%**
Continuation rate for those not at ETS	97.00%	97.00%	97.00%
Number eligible to reenlist	295	303	300
Reenlistments	264	271	268
Number who continue without reenlisting	1,471	1,508	1,496
End of 2nd-period inventory	1,736	1,779	1,764

Both the Delta method and the ACOL 2 approach show that the bonus induces small increases in the first-period retention rate. The Delta method predicts 45 new reenlistments; ACOL 2 predicts 30. In this case, the ACOL 2 method does not show any significant effect on the second-period reenlistment rate.

Temporary Early Retirement Authority (TERA)

The TERA program allowed Air Force personnel to retire at 15 YOS, with retired pay that was a multiple of their base pay. The multiple is 2.5 percent times the YOS, reduced by a factor of (1/12) percent for each month before 20 YOS that the person retired. For enlisted personnel in grade E6 (technical sergeant) at 18 YOS (24 months before achieving 20 YOS), the reduction factor is (24/12) = 2%, so the retirement multiple is (2.5%)(18)(1 – 0.02) = 44.1%. Base pay from the year 2000 pay tables is $24,095, so the annual TERA payment is ($24,095)(0.441) = $10,626. This inducement to leave the Air Force produces a *decrease* in ACOL of about $90,000. Table A.2 compares the Delta method and the ACOL 2 approach in this situation.

38

Table A.2

Effect of TERA on E6s with 18 YOS

	Base	Delta Method	ACOL 2
Initial inventory	6,335	6,335	6,335
% at ETS	14.00%	14.00%	14.00%
Reenlistment rate	**98.70%**	**31.78%**	**50.75%**
Continuation rate for those not at ETS	99.60%	99.60%	99.60%
Number eligible to reenlist	887	887	887
Reenlistments	875	282	450
Number who continue without reenlisting	5,426	5,426	5,426
End of 1st-period inventory	6,302	5,708	5,876
% at ETS	16.30%	16.30%	16.30%
Reenlistment rate	**75.21%**	**75.21%**	**81.81%**
Continuation rate for those not at ETS	97.00%	97.00%	97.00%
Number eligible to reenlist	1,027	930	958
Reenlistments	773	700	784
Number who continue without reenlisting	5,116	4,634	4,771
End of 2nd-period inventory	5,889	5,334	5,555

The Delta method in this case predicts a much larger decrease in the first-period reenlistment rate than the ACOL 2 approach does. Additionally, the ACOL 2 model predicts that the *second*-period reenlistment rate will increase—a change that the Delta method cannot capture. These combined differences mean that at the end of two periods, the Delta method would show a total loss of 1,001 people from the initial inventory, but the ACOL 2 method would show a loss of only 780.

Conclusion

These examples show that for ACOL changes such as those to be expected from reenlistment bonuses, retention changes using the Delta method with ACOL 2 coefficients are fairly close to the "true" ACOL 2 approach. For very large ACOL changes that might be expected from radical changes to retirement policy, the general direction of changes in retention can be determined in the first period of the change, but, compared with the ACOL 2 model, the Delta method will overestimate the effects on retention. In addition, with very large ACOL changes, the Delta method cannot show the potential changes in retention rates in *future* periods that the ACOL 2 approach can predict.

B. Calculation of the Cost of Leaving for a Dynamic Programming Model

Equation (4.4) in Section 4 showed that the "cost of leaving" in the DRM is

$$c_t(\gamma) = w_t^S - w_t^L(t) + \gamma + \beta E_t(U_{t+1}) - \sum_{\tau=t+1}^{T+1} \beta^{\tau-t} w_t^L(\tau). \tag{B.1}$$

It is possible to develop a closed form for this expression that allows a straightforward "backward recursion" calculation of the cost of leaving and shows the close connection with the ACOL model. As described by Daula and Moffitt (1995), if the distribution of random shocks has a mean of zero and a standard deviation σ_ε, the expectation term in equation (B.1) can be expanded as follows:

$$E_t(U_{t+1}) = F\left(\frac{c_{t+1}}{\sigma_\varepsilon}\right)\left(w_{t+1}^S + \gamma + \beta E_{t+1}(U_{t+2})\right) + \left(1 - F\left(\frac{c_{t+1}}{\sigma_\varepsilon}\right)\right)\left(w_{t+1}^L + \sum_{\tau=t+2}^{T+1} \beta^{\tau-t-1} w_{t+1}^L(\tau)\right)$$

$$+ \sigma_\varepsilon f\left(\frac{c_{t+1}}{\sigma_\varepsilon}\right), \tag{B.2}$$

where $F(x)$ is the standard cumulative normal distribution. Equation (B.2) says that the expected value at time t of the best decision at time $t + 1$ is the probability of staying the next period times the value of staying, plus the probability of leaving the next period times the value of leaving plus the extra term

$$\sigma_\varepsilon f\left(\frac{c_{t+1}}{\sigma_\varepsilon}\right).$$

The extra term comes from the fact that in each period the individual will make the "best" choice, so the expected value of the error term associated with staying (see Equation 4.1) will be non-zero. If we define the following expression:

$$r_\tau = \prod_{m=t+1}^{\tau} (\text{Prob}(c_m + \varepsilon_m) > 0)$$

$$= \prod_{m=t+1}^{\tau} F(c_m / \sigma_\varepsilon) = \text{Probability of staying at least until } \tau$$

and assume that $r_t = 1$, then, after considerable algebraic manipulation, we obtain the following expression for the cost of leaving:

$$
\begin{aligned}
c_t(\gamma) = {} & \sum_{\tau=t}^{T} \beta^{\tau-t} r_\tau (w_\tau^S - w_\tau^L) + \sum_{\tau=t}^{T} \beta^{\tau-t} r_\tau \gamma + \sigma_\varepsilon \sum_{\tau=t+1}^{T} \beta^{\tau-t} r_{\tau-1} f\!\left(\frac{c_t}{\sigma_\varepsilon}\right) \\
& + \sum_{\tau=t+1}^{T+1} r_{\tau-1}\!\left[\sum_{z=\tau}^{T+1} \beta^{z-t}(w_\tau^L(z) - w_{\tau-1}^L(z))\right].
\end{aligned}
\tag{B.3}
$$

The cost of leaving consists of three main pieces: a weighted sum of the differences in income from staying and leaving in this and future years, a weighted sum of the taste for staying in the military, and a weighted sum of means of future error terms. The weights come from the probability of staying in each year until τ in order to be in a position to make the comparison of future wage differences, and the sum of the error terms again comes from the fact that future choices made by the individual result in non-zero means of the error term. The last weighted sum in equation (B.3) allows for the possibility that the wages received after leaving the first job may vary depending on when the individual leaves.[1]

As Gotz (1990) and Black, Moffitt, and Warner (1990b) point out, if an individual picked a date to leave based on the maximum ACOL value, he would implicitly assign values of $r_\tau = 1$ to periods before that date and $r_\tau = 0$ to dates thereafter. When this is done, equation (B.3) reduces to the ACOL cost of leaving in expression (2.3) in Section 2, and setting $c_t(\gamma) = 0$ implicitly defines "the level annuity that would make a present-value-of-income maximizing individual indifferent between staying and leaving" (Gotz, 1990, p. 265). Thus, one way of looking at the ACOL model is that it is a version of the DRM in which individuals ignore random shocks.[2]

---

[1]This term is not included in Daula and Moffitt (1995).

[2]The DRM and the ACOL model are connected in more ways than many have realized. Although the formal description of the DRM was published in 1984, development of the ideas was a matter of discussion between Gotz and Warner at least as far back as 1979 (Warner, 1979). Gotz and McCall's unpublished discussion of the DRM goes as far back as 1977. According to Gotz and McCall (1983), Warner's (1979) discussion of the ACOL model for the President's Commission on Military Compensation (*Analysis of the Retention Impact*, 1978) made a reference to their unpublished 1977 work.

Bibliography

Analysis of the Retention Impact of the Proposed Retirement System, Supplementary Papers of the President's Commission on Military Compensation, Washington, DC: U.S. Government Printing Office, April 1978.

Argüden, Yilmaz R., *Personnel Management in the Military: Effects of Retirement Policies on the Retention of Personnel,* Santa Monica, CA: RAND, R-3342-AF, 1986.

Ausink, John A., *The Effect of Changes in Compensation on a Pilot's Decision to Leave the Air Force,* Thesis, Harvard University, Cambridge, MA, 1991.

Black, Matthew, Robert Moffitt, and John T. Warner, "The Dynamics of Job Separation: The Case of Federal Employees," *Journal of Applied Econometrics,* Vol. 5, No. 3, July–August 1990a, pp. 245–262.

———, "Reply to Comment on 'The Dynamics of Job Separation: The Case of Federal Employees,'" *Journal of Applied Econometrics,* Vol. 5, No. 3, July–August 1990b, pp. 269–272.

Butler, J. S., and Robert Moffitt, "A Computationally Efficient Quadrature Procedure for the One-Factor Multinomial Probit Model," *Econometrica,* Vol. 50, No. 3, May 1982, pp. 761–764.

Carnahan, Brice, H. A. Luther, and James O. Wilkes, *Applied Numerical Methods,* New York: John Wiley & Sons, Inc., 1969.

Daula, Thomas, and Robert Moffitt, "Estimating Dynamic Models of Quit Behavior: The Case of Military Reenlistment," *Journal of Labor Economics,* Vol. 13, No. 3, 1995, pp. 499–523.

———, "Estimating a Dynamic Programming Model of Army Reenlistment Behavior" in Curtis L. Gilroy, David K. Horne, and D. Alton Smith, eds., *Military Compensation and Personnel Retention: Models and Evidence,* Alexandria, VA: United States Army Research Institute for the Behavioral and Social Sciences, February 1991.

Fernandez, Richard L., Glenn A. Gotz, and Robert M. Bell, *The Dynamic Retention Model,* Santa Monica, CA: RAND, N-2141-MIL, 1985.

Goldberg, Matthew S., *A Survey of Enlisted Retention: Models and Findings,* Alexandria, VA: Center for Naval Analyses, CRM D0004085.A2/Final, November 2001.

Gotz, Glenn A., "Comment on 'The Dynamics of Job Separation: The Case of Federal Employees,'" *Journal of Applied Econometrics,* Vol. 5, No. 3, July–August 1990, pp. 263–268.

42

Gotz, Glenn A., and John J. McCall, *A Dynamic Retention Model for Air Force Officers: Theory and Estimates,* Santa Monica, CA: RAND, R-3028-AF, 1984.

⸻, "Estimation in Sequential Decision-Making Models: A Methodological Note," *Economics Letters,* Vol. 6, 1980, pp. 131–136.

⸻, *A Sequential Analysis of the Air Force Officer's Retirement Decision,* Santa Monica, CA: RAND, N-1013-1-AF, 1979.

⸻, "Sequential Analysis of the Stay/Leave Decision: US Air Force Officers," *Management Science,* Vol. 29, No. 3, March 1983, pp. 335–351.

Hausman, Jerry A., and David A. Wise, "A Conditional Probit Model for Qualitative Choice: Discrete Decisions Recognizing Interdependence and Heterogeneous Preferences," *Econometrica,* Vol. 46, No. 2, March 1978, pp. 403–426.

Keane, Michael P., and Kenneth I. Wolpin, "The Solution and Estimation of Discrete Choice Dynamic Programming Models by Simulation and Interpolation: Monte Carlo Evidence," *The Review of Economics and Statistics,* Vol. 76, No. 4, November 1994, pp. 648–672.

Kmenta, Jan, *Elements of Econometrics,* 2nd Edition, New York: Macmillan, 1986.

Lumsdaine, Robin L., James H. Stock, and David A. Wise, "Three Models of Retirement: Computational Complexity Versus Predictive Validity," Cambridge, MA: National Bureau of Economic Research, Working Paper No. 3558, December 1990.

Mackin, Patrick C., *Reestimation of ACOL Coefficients for the CAPM Model: Final Report,* Falls Church, VA: SAG Corporation, Project No. HQ0038-4108-0012, August 16, 1996.

Mattock, Michael, unpublished RAND briefing on "Using Simulation to Estimate the Structural Parameters of a Dynamic Retention Model."

Rust, John, *Dealing with the Complexity of Economic Calculations,* New Haven, CT: Yale University, 1997 (invited paper for Fundamental Limits to Knowledge in Economics, Santa Fe Institute, July 31–August 3, 1996), see http://gemini. econ.umd.edu/jrust/papers.html.

Stern, Steven, "Approximate Solutions to Stochastic Dynamic Programs," *Econometric Theory,* Vol. 13, No. 3, June 1997a, p. 392, see "Publications and Working Papers" link at www.people.virginia.edu/~sns5r/.

⸻, "Simulation-Based Estimation," *Journal of Economic Literature,* December 1997b, see "Publications and Working Papers" link at www.people.virginia. edu/~sns5r/.

Stock, James H., and David A. Wise, "Pensions, the Option Value of Work, and Retirement," *Econometrica,* Vol. 58, No. 5, September 1990, pp. 1151–1180.

Varian, Hal R., *Microeconomic Analysis,* 2nd Edition, New York: W. W. Norton & Company, 1984.

Warner, John T., *Alternative Military Retirement Systems: Their Effects on Enlisted Retention*, Alexandria, VA: Center for Naval Analyses, September 1979.

Warner, John T., and Beth J. Asch, "The Economics of Military Manpower," in Keith Hartley and Todd Sandler, eds., *Handbook of Defense Economics*, Volume I, New York: Elsevier, 1995.

Wolpin, Kenneth I., "Public Policy Uses of Discrete-Choice Dynamic Programming Models," *The American Economic Review*, Vol. 86, No. 2, Papers and Proceedings of the Hundredth and Eighth Annual Meeting of the American Economic Association, San Francisco, January 5–7, 1996 (May 1996), pp. 427–432.